the window on the train

POEMS BY: J.P.

POCKET EDITION

Copyright © 2025 by Moonlit Paper Press

All rights reserved. No part of this publication may be reproduced, distributed, or transmitted in any form or by any means, including photocopying, recording, or other electronic or mechanical methods, without the prior written permission of the publisher, except in the case of brief quotations used in reviews or other noncommercial uses permitted by copyright law.

For permission requests or bulk orders, please contact:

IngramSpark / Ingram Content Group
ingramsparksupport@ingramcontent.com
1 Ingram Blvd.
La Vergne, Tennessee 37086
USA

ISBN: 978-1-0697973-0-8

Pocket Edition
Distributed by IngramSpark

Cover and interior designed by the author
✉ moonlitpaperpress@gmail.com

the window on the train

for the record:
i was here

the window on the train

contents:

what's the point………..………………..5
what i wrote in autumn……………….7
what i wrote in winter……………......21
what i wrote in spring……..………...35
what i wrote in summer..…………....51
what i wrote on the train…..……......60

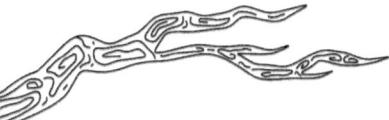

WHAT'S THE POINT

life is not
a linear thing
one day heals
the next day stings

a back and forth
a tug of war
of love and loss
and what it's for

so these are not
the softest words
and rarely tell
of singing birds

while sometimes sweet
they've got more edge
they poke for fun
and walk a ledge

they tease and play
between the lines
with serious notes
and silly rhymes

but even though
they're often rough
they are my truth
and that's enough

the window on the train

they came in fall
when i was lost
and carried me
through winter's frost

then spring and summer
in the rain
and at the window
on the train

they more than often
make me cry
but i have to write
or i will die

dramatic
yes
but also true
it's what we poets
have to do

so here are my words
in the raw
of things i did
and felt
and saw

they serve no purpose
but to give
a record of
a year i lived

autumn

the window on the train

LEAVES IN AUTUMN

i think it is the saddest thing to know
that leaves in autumn do not ever show
their true colors until they begin to die
perhaps they are a lot like you and i

NATURE IS MY FAVOURITE POET

looking out my window
i can read her verses every hour
written in the sky
projected on this fading horizon
when i see the fallen branch upon
the ground
universal truths of life and of death
reveal themselves to me

i am a plagiarist

these words are not my own
they belong to her
nature
my favourite poet

the window on the train

FAULT LINES

there are cracks in the ground
where we used to lie in warmth
but these crevices
are seeded with truth
and baptized by hard rain
so come spring
they will bear flowers
and at last reveal
the earnest truth
that we often see growth
in all the places
that have been broken

AN OLD WINDOW

in our house
there will be an old window
not the type that leaks
or lets in the cold air
the sturdy kind
of many panes
the sort you would imagine
has held in the warmth
of a dozen lifetimes
and immeasurable love

it will keep us safe
and shield us from the storm
all our lives

SOLSTICE

sleep now
soon it will be
the season of transformation
a chapter to recall
that everything must perish
in order to begin anew
so rest a while
and let this slow autumn haze
turn you over again
and enter the world of dreams

NOTHING MUCH

let's do *nothing* together

sit beneath the trees

visit our favourite park

watch the autumn leaves
glue themselves like paper mache
to the dampened ground

sip something warm
from a paper cup
as winter comes around

soon it will be too cold here
to sit and watch and wait
so let's do *nothing* soon my love
before it gets too late

the window on the train

REMEMBERING US

the seasons turn
from green to gold
and in the cold
the crisp air holds
the loose strands
of my auburn hair
as i quietly stare
and think about
when love was new

it's always raining
when i think of you

and i ask myself
now that we're apart:

were we a tragedy
or a work of art?

MADNESS

there's a different kind of madness
that comes at night:
do you know it?

something happens in the absence of
light
that makes me feel alive
i thrive in the darkness
the gloom
the fog
others might get bogged down
by the cold shadows that come out
to play
but to me they are home
i beg them to stay
they give me inspiration
and comfort
and air
they tell me the truth
when there's no one there

in the dark i find peace
and i can finally see
because there's no one around
and i can be me

i am not mad
i am finally free

NOTE TO SELF

do not follow your heart
if it only calls at night
or breaks through peaceful dreams
just to say: *you're not doing it right*

do not follow your heart
if it calls you from your home
to be aimless or to roam
through vast deserts
of new beginnings
and countless non-adventures
forsaking all you own
everything you've known
mother
father
brother
wife
loyal friend
all your life

true adventures are always marked
with beginnings and with ends
and returning to old friends
who see you on and greet you back
from the wild and unbeaten track

it is never a new truth you find
but a tired one as old as time

the window on the train

your heart is a gentle
and quiet sound
that will always leave
you homeward bound

so if you are being forced
down steep valleys
and up sharp peaks
do not follow your heart

it is not your heart that speaks

I AM CHANGE

what i felt yesterday
i do not feel today
and what i am today
i will not be tomorrow
but i will live my life
with conviction
every hour
trusting that
no matter the circumstance
my average dealing
will equal truth

the window on the train

EXPERIENCE

the flowers in your hair
may have fallen to the ground
scattered here and there
never to be found again
but they have left their truth
along your weary path
and in their aftermath
seed the promise of yesterday's
deeds
and wait in the weeds
to grant that you will bloom
tomorrow

winter

the window on the train

ICE STORM

sitting here beneath the january sky
the crystal branches cry
weeping under the weight
of nature's frozen kiss
and all at once in this
i am both heaviness and light
and overwhelmed and right
as i breathe the quiet air
a snowy owlet's stare
and the steadiness
of my own solitary breath
is all that is there

THE BEGINNING OF THE END

something has been lost
in the way that the frost
lingers in the air
between your breath and mine
while the dim sunshine
falls off the bay
and seems to say
the day is done
though we haven't begun
to see the change
we only feel a little strange

the window on the train

MY EVERYTHING

if i had more than one life
to surrender to love
it would be yours

but i cannot give you
what i do not have

so while this is not
my entirety
i assure you
it's everything
that's left

ULTRAVIOLET

the light is blue and so am i
as evening falls upon the sky
i breathe you in with one last sigh
darkness calls
the stars
they spy and tell a tale of passers-by
the end of love is drawing nigh
the light is blue and so am i

YOU DO NOT COMPLETE ME

here we are again

two broken bodies

trying to find solace in each other's open spaces

but we are two halves from different places

we do not make a whole

perhaps we must find these missing pieces on our own

and then one day we can return
to meet once again
for the very first time

PERSPECTIVE

i was angry with the night
for betraying the light
and turning its shoulder
on what was right
but i spoke too soon
because that afternoon
i saw the sun
revealing the moon
so it is not so stark
for the song of the lark
was the first to strike
and betray the dark

ANXIOUS AND AVOIDANT

falling in love with you
was like diving headfirst
into a sea of glass
the days would pass
and i removed the shards
one by one
but when i was done
more would appear
out of thin air
crowding my lungs
and reminding me
that i no longer remember
how to breathe

DISSOCIATION

i started on this train of thought
more eager than i should
and now i'm drifting off to space
i feel misunderstood
my words they briefly cling the air
then fall to the spaces between
you're giving me a hard blank stare
and you don't know what i mean
i'm dearly grasping on to place
and time and circumstance
but something left me with no trace
and i am in a trance

the window on the train

DO NOT LOOK FOR ME

do not look for me if you do not
mean it
if you are bored
if you are wanting nothing more
than to pass the time
if you can no longer carry
the sound of your own heartbeat
alone
if you are tired
unsatisfied
desperate
finished
if you are needing someone
to help you kill the remaining hours
of a wasted life
do not look for me

i will not be there

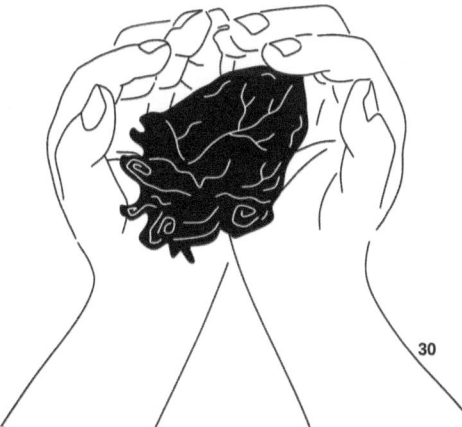

CLOWN SCHOOL

do not be ashamed of what you feel
we are all born knowing how to love
the right way
then we encounter those
who have been taught
the wrong lessons of love
taught to use and not to give
taught conditions of love
but deep down you always knew
the right way to love
so keep your heart open
through this ache
and never again
take a masterclass from a fool

the window on the train

THE STARS WERE OUR WITNESS

i think of you
when i look at the stars

not because they are bright
or brave
or pure
or magic

but because they were there
when we were there

and each endless night
that engulfed our love
was pinned to my heart over again

i think of you
when i look at the stars
because now they are all that is left

PAIN

i will always
choose this pain
rather than feel
nothing at all

it will let me
love again

and again

and again

WINTER LOVE

as i kissed
the last frost of winter
off your lashes
late that february evening
the snow turned to rain
and i thought to myself
how funny it was
that in a mere
matter of moments
a stranger could grow
to mean so much

spring

RUSTIC LIFE

i do not like
clean lines or smooth edges
i like life best
with a bit of patina on it
the cracks
are how the light gets in
as they say
so give me all the spaces
between the lines
and i will dance
and live in truth

MISUNDERSTOOD

please
misunderstand me
get me wrong
make many assumptions
about my character
tell the tribe
spread rumors
with your ignorant tongue

this is my preference

because every time you try to "get"
what i am about
i become a slave
to all the masks
you try to make me wear

WRITER'S BLOCK

as i'm clawing at the pages
my finger catches an edge
the words spill out like madness
as i teeter on the ledge
the insanity is stable
as i bleed my truth like wine
but something stops me in my tracks
and i can't find the line
i want to draw your attention
but my pen is out of ink
i try to write you pretty prose
but instead take up a drink

RUMINATION

i call to you softly sometimes
when i am alone
just to feel the words on my tongue
to taste you again
through rituals of life
in moments of rest
through coffee cups
i whisper
spinning spoons
like a trance
the aroma of life
rises to my lips
and i say your name

the window on the train

i am on a voyage
as darkness falls upon this day
a journey to the self
an expedition to the soul

DEAR HYPOCRITE

you can write these famous words
in hardened ink
mark the walls within your home
with what you think
adorn your pillowcases
with fine lace
and etch your skin
with passages of grace

but remember this one very
important thing
about the golden manuscripts
you bring:

these words are nothing more
than screams at night
lucid dreams
and fantasies of flight
that do not count
if from the very start
you fail to carry them
within your heart

PRETTY PRIVILEGE

i'm in big trouble
but i am dimple-cheeked
and button-nosed

they tell me it's a good thing:
the reason they didn't
toss the baby with the bathwater
when all hell broke loose

but now this neoteny deceives

they like the way
i smile with my eyes
but i am wincing too
they cannot tell
that these are not laugh lines

TOO DEEP

my dear
you are far too deep
to be drowning
in such shallow waters

take a second look
at your reflection in the tide
try not to hide
your true feelings anymore
dig your heels into the sand
and remind yourself
that you know how to stand

the window on the train

LOW-HANGING FRUIT

i grab the nearest apple
and i crush it with my teeth
these hanging fruit are sweet
i search hungrily for another
it is already at my feet
now easier to reach
i stoop to meet its level
lying on the floor
it collapses in my grip
it is rotted to the core

FAILING TO FIT

there are too many people here

herds of people
hordes of people
all doing the same thing

i want desperately to join them
they would like that too
but their movements
are foreign to me
their purpose eludes
i do not think i will ever be the same

i mimic them for a while

how can i fit into a crowd
when i was always set apart

was i born to stand alone?

CONVENIENCE

fake plants
do not die
but they also
do not grow

SILENT SCREAM

you do not have to scream
at the top of your lungs
just to tell the truth

a whisper is fine
and actions more loud

but voiceless words
fall on blinded eyes
when you keep the company
of those who cannot see

the window on the train

BIRD TEST

if i peeled you an orange
would you notice me

how about a cup of tea
what if i made a pot for two
we could even watch it brew
together as we sat and laughed
seeing all the nature pass
at the window sill

if i mentioned the beautiful bill
on the morning bird
would you hear a single word

or would you miss me as you do
because of your careless
and narrow view
as you wondered in an idle flash:

who left the fruit peel in the trash?

LOVE IN YOUR TWENTIES

it's the little things that stay with me now:

i remember the decrepit apartment
above the laundromat
i remember how we managed to find
love there for the first time
i remember how it felt to fall asleep
beneath the crooked ceiling fan and
pretend that our dreams weren't just
dreams
i remember how it was always a little
cold and a little damp and how the
white noise of the dehumidifier
would lull us to sleep
i remember how nothing was
bothersome then

you never need much at first do you?

a single bed perhaps
a sturdy floor
and a slow deep slumber
under the trapped light
of too many stars

do you remember when this was
enough to keep our love?

the window on the train

LONGING IS LIGHT/ LOVING IS HEAVY

i can still recall
the bright april morning
when i was still light with longing
before the weight of love
filled my being
for the very first time

now there is a heaviness
i will always choose to carry

this sacred burden
this thankless promise
this unconditional desire
has given my life meaning
where there once was none

summer

NEW LOVE

it was just about june
when the morning moon
kissed the pond
and i grew quite fond
of the way that your shoes
of sapphire blues
remained on the shore
askew by the door
always next to mine

SEASONS IN THE SUN

the flowers by my bedside
must have something to say
because somehow
they still face the light
when wilted
dead
and gray

maybe in the end
they recalled their vibrant youth
and basked in sunshine in their
hearts
and realized deeper truth

so when it's our last goodbye
i hope we won't be sad
and like the daisies on the sill
let memories make us glad

CALIFORNIA SHUTTERS

i can still remember
the way the evening sun
would cast a golden shadow
on our love
through the shades
onto the floor
your body
bathed in light
where we were

THE SPACES BETWEEN

i think of you at the beginning
of every day
i still see your face at the end
of every night
in the spaces between
when there's no one around
when there isn't a sound
but the beating of my restless heart
so when we're apart
and you find yourself reaching
for me
across the sea of this separation
you can meet me in that place
where it is always dusk
and always dawn
where memory lives
you will find me there
in the shadow of life
in the remains of the day

i never left

THE ONE

i do not believe in "the one"
because it makes no logical sense
yet there is something
different with you
and the feeling is more intense

i do not believe in soulmates
or signs from up above
but there's no denying
you'll always be
my favourite person to love

TRUE LOVE

i'd write of stardust in your eyes
or flowers that bloom in arid dirt

but you my love are more alive
in every way more down to earth

i cannot touch you in the sky
or reach across a vast dead sea

so i will meet you eye to eye
and you can stay in love with me

BEAUTIFULLY BROKEN (KINTSUGI)

maybe you weren't meant
to leave here unbroken
maybe the scars on your heart
are truth spoken
like a map of light
leading others out of the dark
perhaps this is how
you will make your mark
and maybe you haven't
lost your genuine smile
because you live a life
that makes all this suffering
worthwhile

FORTITUDE

this world will try to break you
mold and shape you
force you into being
something you are not
crashing and colliding
exploding and pressing
there is no escaping
the inevitable chaos
so i say let it smash you
let it take you down
let it pummel you
and when it does
bend into the light
shift and adapt
learn the hard lessons
that life has to teach
but never let it touch your core
because when it is all said and done
you can rest in the knowledge
that no matter how difficult life became
you did not let it change you
you did not give in
and in every instant
you lived in truth
and were unmoved

the window on the train

on the train
notes, musings & quotes from my travels

when i said forever
i only meant it if you stayed

there is too much time now

forever is too long
if you are not here

the window on the train

you cannot break off
pieces of yourself
to make them whole

but you can certainly
die trying

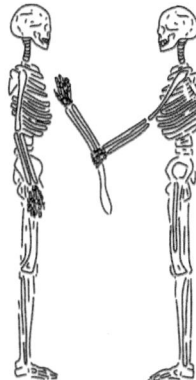

love:
it was easy the first time 'round
but now
it is the most courageous thing
you will ever do

— second love

the window on the train

time will not be
discounted
would you rather
pay for it now
or later

the way you've allowed
the dust to settle
on this uncorked wine
makes me think
you're here to stay

                              – recovery

this potion dulls the senses
all my edges
once rough
are now sanded smooth
i am tufted
i have become the wall
padding the home
of my latent shadow self

      – relapse

the window on the train

to the ones who left:

you did not teach me
how to love
but i learned to love
because of you

am i an underachiever
or am i merely satisfied
by simpler deeds?

the window on the train

i can only love
as deeply as i live

i love you

it hit me in an instant
not like lightning
all at once
but rather
it was like a feeling
i've always known

comparison is the thief of joy

we may not be all that special
or different from the rest
but here
in this corner of life
in our own private universe
perhaps we can find a way
to see just this
and have that be enough

you are angry because
love is not the fairy tale
they said it would be
but what if i told you
it could be so much more

the window on the train

my soft heart does not
make me weak

believe this:

i will fight you
even with tears
in my eyes

face your fears
your demons
have only one
worthy adversary

the window on the train

some comforts
are too comfortable
so i find comfort
in the uncomfortable

when you take down your stars
so the dim can shine more bright
all you do is make it impossible
for either of you to see

the window on the train

your love is worth the wait
and worth the weight

you cannot control
who you love
but you can decide
how you let them
carry your heart

the window on the train

you can see a lifetime in her hands
it's not so much
that they reveal to you her age
rather
they tell of her experience

it may have taken
more than one spring
for this growth to flower
but at last
i can no longer see
the forest floor

the window on the train

beauty was her curse
the mask she wore
all her life

you are not changing
you are becoming

the window on the train

sometimes the words
feel better than they sound

say them anyway

what is the sound the soul makes
if no one is around to hear it?

the window on the train

looks can be deceiving
and sometimes that means
you get a bargain

our love was never
black and white
but it was always
more black than white

the window on the train

i miss you sometimes
but then i meet someone
who can see more of my light
and i forget your name

never trust a man
who claims to have
no vice

i suspect he betrays
even himself

rather

give me a man
who knows his demons well
and has them wrestled
into submission

the window on the train

the lump you feel
in your throat
when you can't let go
of the tears
is the knowledge that
you are not yet safe

trust that feeling

when i saw the spark die
in your eyes that night
i'm afraid there wasn't enough
of a flame left in mine
to keep us both alive

the window on the train

am i in a rut
or have i finally
found my home?

today i found my self again
it was in the most familiar of places

the window on the train

is there anything as peculiar
as when nature herself
is out of season

you call it crazy
i call it
the only truth
i've ever known

the window on the train

it's going to end
in tragedy

try harder to laugh

– life

i wish that my mind
were as tired as my body

the window on the train

this memory is heavy
and too hard to hold
but it is all i have left

i feasted on your crumbs –
to me there were mountains

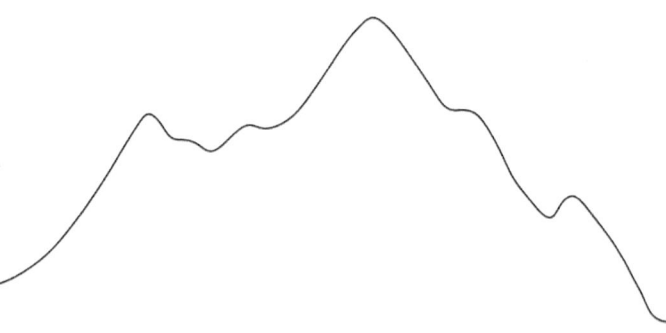

the window on the train

you will never have
what you want
until you want
what you have

there is nothing more extraordinary
than a soul with the courage
to live an ordinary life

the window on the train

in this uninhabitable place
you gave all of yourself
to love
the only way
you knew how
do not think
that it went
unnoticed

– karma

every journey outward is a journey inward.
what reflections from the road deserve to be remembered?
an image, perhaps? a poem of your own?
now dear reader, it's your turn...

the window on the train

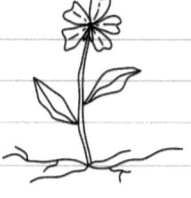

www.ingramcontent.com/pod-product-compliance
Lightning Source LLC
Chambersburg PA
CBHW020341010526
44119CB00048B/563